MW00606200

Mental Health & Gen Z

What *Educators* Need to Know

Springtide
RESEARCH INSTITUTE®

A SPRINGTIDE
A PROMISE.

TO YOU

. . . who are young, full of wonder and possibility. You who are navigating some of life's most important questions and most tumultuous waters. You who are sometimes flourishing and sometimes floundering and oftentimes both. You who are at once being and becoming.

> We dedicate our work to your thriving.

> We dedicate ourselves to understanding your inner and outer lives.

TO YOU

. . . who are fiercely devoted to young people. You who advocate for and walk alongside young people with steadiness. You who are unwavering amid the waves.

> We offer our research as an aid to the role you already play.

> We offer ourselves as allies in accompaniment.

TRIBUTE.
A PLEDGE.

 AND TO

. . . the waves that crash, the currents that bend and beckon, the dark depths, and the effervescent crests. To this all-important period of life: worthy of considered listening and faithful retelling, worthy of companionship, worthy of care.

We situate our work at this intersection of human and religious experience in the lives of young people: a space of ebb and flow, of calm and chaos, of clear and murky moments.

A space we are dedicated to exploring and engaging

 WITH YOU.

This report is part of *The Springtide Series on Mental Health*. In this report, we rely on a data set of over 4,000 surveys, with more than 3,000 completed by students, and 80 in-depth interviews with a specific focus on mental health in schools and educational settings. Future reports and resources in the series will focus on how families, religious communities, and workplaces can foster young people's mental and emotional well-being.

The series emphasizes stories young people share in interviews—not just statistics from surveys. Our survey research enables us to reach a nationally representative group of young people and report on quantifiable trends. Our interviews enable us to discern nuances embedded in the details of young people's lives. Taken together, these two types of data illuminate the needs of young people and ways organizational leaders might be able to help.

S THE SPRINGTIDE SERIES ON MENTAL HEALTH 2022

CONTENTS

Interested in reflecting on this report with more depth and guidance? *A Guide to Turn the Tide* presents a series of reflections and prompts designed to be used by individuals or small groups, or as the foundation for large-group workshops and conversations, as you journey through *Mental Health & Gen Z: What Educators Need to Know.*

FROM SPRINGTIDE'S EXECUTIVE DIRECTOR

In the past decade, many teachers (myself included) have been trained to spot the warning signs of mental-health crises in our students, direct them toward resources, and check in on them regularly—all while doing the thousands of other things that constitute our jobs.

And sometimes it works. Sometimes we catch students just in time. Just before they fall. We can't focus too long on the vivid alternative, but instead sigh with relief that some tragedy did not unfold, at least not today.

But sometimes it doesn't work. We don't see. We're too busy or too untrained or the situation is simply beyond our capacity to see and respond to.

I've been on both sides. I've worked with students who have told me later that my plea that they get help, and my assistance connecting them to that help, saved their life. And I've lost students to suicide just months before graduation.

In both cases, I couldn't help but think to myself: *"This isn't what I was trained to do."*

But like you, I couldn't just sit and watch an epidemic unfold in my classroom and on my campus, day in and day out, without trying to do something. Even if that something never felt like enough.

The research we're doing about mental health is, in many ways, a passion project for me. For years, I've longed for a way to begin building an organizational culture at a school or university that is designed, at its very core, to be mental-health friendly, rather than amended, as an afterthought, to respond to mental-health crises.

"This report is the tool that I wish my campus had when I was a professor."

—Dr. Josh Packard

This report is the tool that I wish my campus had when I was a professor. It is intended to sit alongside crisis intervention and early indicator training and hopefully prevent reliance on crisis response tools. We believe, and our data confirm, that more prepared cultures can address mental-health issues before they become mental-health crises.

In fall 2021, our Research Advisory Board convened with our staff to talk about the direction this focus on mental health would take us in 2022. Before we began discussing the logistics and themes, each member offered the first name of a young person in their life who has been impacted by this epidemic. We paused together in a moment of silence to hold those young people, and those unnamed, in our hearts, in our thoughts, or in our prayers, each practicing a reverence suited to our own systems of beliefs, but a reverence nonetheless shared and expressed as a common concern for these young people and a wish for their well-being.

This report, and this series, is for them.

Josh Packard, PhD

As you read and work, please drop us a line *@WeAreSpringtide* on Facebook, Instagram, or Twitter and use *#MentalHealthandGenZ* to start the conversation. Learn more at *springtideresearch.org* and let us know how you're helping create mental-health friendly organizations for young people.

INTRODUCTION

The mental-health crisis among young people has reached epidemic proportions. The American Academy of Pediatrics, the Children's Hospital Association, and the American Academy of Child and Adolescent Psychiatry recently declared this crisis a national emergency. Widely available data confirm high rates of depression, anxiety, violence, and suicide among young people. Our own data tell the same story:

57% of young people say **they have experienced trauma.**

34% of young people tell us when it comes to their mental health, they are **not flourishing**.

In interviews, young people tell us that isolation and loneliness became huge concerns for them during the pandemic. They tell us of crushing pressure to get good grades so they can go to college and pursue a meaningful career. They say that seeing others' successes on social media can bring them down. They tell us they feel like they are living on a dying planet. They say finding purpose is difficult sometimes.

Whether school environments exacerbate or mitigate these stressors, young people no doubt *bring* stress, tension, depression, and anxiety about these and other issues to their classrooms.

Educators are aware of this. Many incredible initiatives are underway, especially in schools. Leaders are responding to students in crisis. They are equipping adults and students with mental-health "first-aid" training. What's more, psychologists and therapists are helping individuals learn how to improve their own mental health.

At Springtide, we aren't psychologists or guidance counselors. We aren't child development experts. We are sociologists dedicated to listening to young people ages 13 to 25. Our sociological lens allows us to see two gaps, amid the many gains, when it comes to mental-health initiatives today.

> **First**, the current crisis puts the attention on how to respond to young people's immediate health needs. That's good and necessary. But what's missing is sufficient attention to long-term, proactive strategies to keep young people's minds healthy.

> **Second**, mental-health initiatives center largely on the individual and the psychological: What can *you* be doing differently to improve *your* mental health? That's good and necessary too. But what's missing is attention to structural factors that affect mental well-being: What can organizations do to better support the mental health of young people?

These two gaps helped us define our research questions. We wanted to know: What qualities make youth-serving organizations mental-health friendly? To answer this, we turned to decades of sociological research. We found three all-important qualities of such organizations: They enable social connections, they communicate achievable expectations, and they help young people develop a sense of purpose. Then we set out to answer this question: What strategies help leaders enhance these qualities within their organizations?

Crisis Prevention, Not Crisis Response

Many schools are focused on responding to the immediate mental-health needs of young people—and for good reason. Data from Inseparable, an organization lobbying for policy shifts in national mental-health care, emphasize the critical role of educators:

> Investments in prevention and early intervention . . . pay immediate dividends, create significant savings down the line, and ultimately help keep our kids alive. **Of students receiving mental health services, roughly 30% find that support in schools, making our education system the most accessed mental-health delivery system by children and adolescents.**

But the epidemic proportions of this crisis suggest that more is needed. Initiatives that *prevent* mental-health struggles are as important as those that respond to young people in crisis. Plenty of organizations work to create safe spaces or to shift rhetoric around mental illness and stigma, but *many* organizations, including schools, still default to a response that amounts to preparation for the instances when a mental-health *concern* becomes a mental-health *crisis*.

Reacting to the immediate needs of young people in crisis is essential—but it is not enough. In fact, 22-year-old university student Lana speaks to a theme that emerged in our interviews: Young people are frustrated when schools focus on crisis response rather than prevention. She and other young people we interviewed called these reactions *performative mental-health resources*.

> "[In] my university context, performative mental-health resources, especially those that aren't long-term, do more harm than good. So bringing in dogs to pet at the library common floor during finals **does not address the core element of why students have an uptick in hotline calls and stress and anxiety, like crippling anxiety, during finals** and the two weeks leading up to [them]. Therapy dogs aren't going to solve that. [Instead, we need] consistent mental-health resources that [address] how academia is structured to make students stressed."

Studies demonstrate that petting animals (especially in university settings during intense periods like final exams) *can* and *does* reduce stress among students, even if briefly. But young people express frustration when school initiatives don't also address the underlying reasons for stress—namely, the stressors that *come from* school. Lana goes on:

> "They do all of this as a performative measure to show that the school thinks and cares about mental health. To some extent, I know the people who organize it and I really appreciate it—like I would rather they *do* that than *not*. And the dogs are really cute. But **I would really, really urge them to think more long-term and less performative because what those little bouts of mental-health resources look like [to me] is *inconsistency*. It's inconsistent, and frankly, [it's] doing more for the university's image rather than the well-being of their students.** I think [it's] a reactive measure. I'm like, *'Ooh, A for effort, but D for motivation, and probably less for impact.'*"

> —Lana, 22

Educators and leaders within educational institutions undoubtedly already value proactive initiatives that support mental wellness before young people are in crisis. Inevitably, schools must meet *immediate, urgent* needs. But what can be done to help *prevent* mental unwellness among students in the first place? How do we create a scenario where therapy dogs aren't *needed* in the library during finals? Young people themselves sense that while these efforts are *good*, they are not *good enough*.

I think [it's] a reactive measure. I'm like, *'Ooh, A for effort, but D for motivation, and probably less for impact.'*

—Lana, 22

Creating Organizations That Are Mental-Health Friendly: *Focusing on Connection, Expectations, and Purpose*

The issues that impact young people's mental health are broad, ranging from the macro (climate change, social media, stress from school, political polarization) to the personal (school, home, friends). The solution must engage this broad array of social issues. Noah, 24, articulates a concern that surfaced in our interviews; namely, that "there needs to be big structural changes" and that leaders can't "just tell people to make individual changes" when it comes to improving mental health.

Noah goes on: "Adults, especially those who have money and the time to really campaign for something, should spend at least as much time doing that as they do trying to tell young people [to find support systems]." For Noah, the responsibility adults have is not just to mentor young people through their mental-health concerns, but to vote to expand health care or to lobby for financial accessibility around insurance premiums for mental-health care.

The national conversation about mental health is right in shifting *away* from the individual and the psychological—that is, what can one person be doing differently to improve their own mental health—and beginning to reframe the issue as a collective concern: What can *organizations and groups—indeed, what can schools*—be doing to better support the mental health of their students?

Schools that create connection, foster alignment between tools and expectations, and help young people discover a sense of purpose are highly likely to succeed at promoting the mental health and flourishing of young people.

>

CONNECTION *is about relationships. Within schools, strong connections lead to a sense of belonging. Our data show that for young people, sensing that they're noticed, feeling named, and being known in school correlates with having a sense of belonging with mental wellness. Helping young people make connections that lead to belonging at school is a proactive way to mitigate mental illness. Our data here uncovered some ways to accomplish this.*

Students who feel they belong at school say they are "flourishing a lot" in their mental health at higher rates than those who do not feel they belong.

 EXPECTATIONS *are the standards that young people feel pressure to meet or exceed in order to succeed. These can be explicit or implicit. If expectations at school are unachievable or unclear, young people will often judge themselves rather than the standards negatively, causing their mental health to suffer. Our data show that making sure young people have the right tools to meet expectations is a matter of clear communication and accessible resources.*

Students who agree they have the tools they need for success say they are "flourishing a lot" in their mental health at higher rates than those who feel otherwise.

 PURPOSE *at schools is about helping young people connect with something bigger than themselves. This can be a subject they're passionate about, a community they're involved with, a spiritual practice that grounds them, or more. Though fewer young people turn to religious institutions for conversations about meaning, they nonetheless need spaces that help them discover a sense of purpose. Our data show that schools—with professionals trained and passionate about exposing young people to new ideas and possibilities—are central places for this critical work.*

Students who agree that school is a place that helps them discover their purpose say they are "flourishing a lot" in their mental health at higher rates than those who feel otherwise.

We need organizations— in particular, we need schools— that are intentionally structured to be mental-health friendly.

Schools are at the forefront of innovative mental-health initiatives. And with good reason. Teachers, administrators, coaches, counselors, professors, and staff meet young people during some of their most formative years. Springtide has data to help institutions and individuals enhance the mental-health efforts that are already well underway. As always, our data are collected and analyzed in ways designed to make ideas for taking action clear. We don't need more hand-wringing about the state of young people's mental health. We need proactive approaches to crisis prevention. We need organizations—in particular, we need schools—that are intentionally structured to be mental-health friendly.

This report offers qualitative and quantitative data that reflect students' experiences of connection, expectation, and purpose. First, in our Key Findings, we present an overview of how young people are faring mentally at school. In the chapters that follow, we offer data and tips for fostering belonging, creating alignment around expectations, and cultivating a sense of purpose *for* young people while they are in your care at schools.

We're leveraging our research capabilities to help educational leaders leverage their institutional resources, all with one goal: to accomplish organizational and social changes that can increase the mental-health friendliness of schools. Perhaps, then, the *performative*—to use Lana's term—or *reactive* efforts around mental health won't be needed at all.

The Voices of Young People Podcast

Season 7 of *The Voices of Young People Podcast* will feature perspectives, stories, and voices of **16 young people**, in dialogue with Marte Aboagye, Springtide's Head of Community Engagement, and with one another, **in the course of 8 episodes** released throughout the year as part of our *Springtide Series on Mental Health*.

Guests in this season range in age from 14 to 25 (ninth grade to young professionals); they represent different parts of the country, different ethnicities, different faith identities, and more. And they're all spending time talking to Springtide—and to you—about Gen Z and mental health.

Tune in throughout 2022 to hear their thoughts on prompts like . . .

Where do you get your messages about mental health?

If you were worried about your own or your friend's mental health, who would you turn to? And what is it about that relationship that helps you know they're trustworthy?

In what ways do you feel connected to something bigger than yourself? Does this sense of purpose play a role in your mental health?

What makes you feel like you matter when you're at school?

Find the latest episodes of this powerful season wherever you get your podcasts, including Google Podcasts, Anchor, Apple Podcasts, Spotify, or our website:

springtideresearch.org/community/podcast

Mental Health & Gen Z
AT SCHOOL

57% of young people say **they have experienced trauma**.

43% say they **don't feel they are living fully**.

34% of young people tell us when it comes to their mental health, they are **not flourishing**.

Young people experience different rates of mental healthiness at different levels of school.

*Percent of young people who say they are **not flourishing** in their mental health:*

Level	Percent
High school	34%
College	31%
Middle school	29%
Trade school	28%
Graduate school	23%

High schoolers are more likely than other students to report poor mental health.

S THE SPRINGTIDE SERIES ON MENTAL HEALTH

© 2022 Springtide. Cite, share, and join the conversation at *springtideresearch.org*.

SPRINGTIDE KEY FINDINGS

While young people value seeing a therapist who shares their basic values, *not* sharing identity markers isn't likely to make them hesitate.

▶ **71%** agree or strongly agree that it's important that mental-health services are offered in their native language.

Nearly 60% say it doesn't matter if they share the same racial or ethnic background as their counselor/therapist.

Reasons young people hesitate to see a therapist

Parents don't take concerns about their students' mental health seriously
45%

Religious differences
33%

Ethnic or racial differences from the people available to them at school
32%

Young people of color are more likely than white young people to agree or strongly agree with the statement below:

"It would be important to me that a mental-health counselor share the same racial or ethnic background as me." ▼

57% Black/African American
48% Asian
47% Hispanic/Latino
35% White

There are many reasons young people don't take advantage of the resources provided by schools for mental-health response—despite perhaps needing those resources.

This report focuses not on adding crisis or first-aid resources to the stockpile already available to students, but rather on creating environments that are more mental-health friendly at their very core.

Mental Health & Gen Z
CONNECTION

One of the ways to create schools that are mental-health friendly from the ground up is to focus on connection and to build belonging. Students who feel they belong at school say they are "flourishing a lot" in their mental health at higher rates than those who do not feel they belong.

 Connection matters for mental health.

Overall, schools are doing a good job helping young people feel connected in some basic ways:

71%
Adults acknowledge my presence at my school.

78%
At least one person says hello to me every day.

But there's room for improvement:

Students who "agree" or "strongly agree" with the following statements:

18%
I feel safe enough to talk about what really matters to me.

41%
I have at least one adult that I trust at my school.

S THE SPRINGTIDE SERIES ON MENTAL HEALTH

SPRINGTIDE KEY FINDINGS

How do you feel at school?

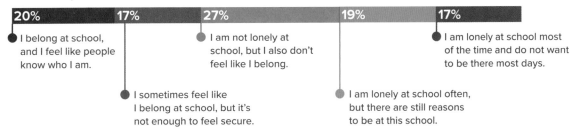

| 20% | 17% | 27% | 19% | 17% |

- **20%** I belong at school, and I feel like people know who I am.
- **17%** I sometimes feel like I belong at school, but it's not enough to feel secure.
- **27%** I am not lonely at school, but I also don't feel like I belong.
- **19%** I am lonely at school often, but there are still reasons to be at this school.
- **17%** I am lonely at school most of the time and do not want to be there most days.

More than 1 in 3 young people tell us they feel lonely at school often or most of the time.

More than 1 in 4 tell us they neither feel lonely nor feel they belong.

Which students feel they belong (or not) at school?

I am lonely at school often or most of the time, by gender:

56%	Nonbinary
38%	Female-identifying
32%	Male-identifying

I belong and feel known at school, by race:

22%	White
21%	Asian
19%	Hispanic or Latino
17%	Black or African American

I am lonely at school often or most of the time, by attendance at a religiously affiliated school or not:

25%	Affiliated
37%	Not affiliated

More than half of nonbinary young people say they feel lonely at school often or most of the time, followed by almost 2 in 5 females and about 1 in 3 males. Young people of color are less likely to feel they belong and are known at school than white young people, though no young people—of any race or ethnicity—say they belong at school at high rates. Attending a religiously affiliated school correlates with a considerably lower sense of loneliness at school than attending a school with no religious affiliation.

Mental Health & Gen Z
EXPECTATIONS

Another key factor in creating schools that are mental-health friendly from the ground up is to make sure expectations and tools are aligned. Students who agree they have the tools they need for success say they are "flourishing a lot" in their mental health at higher rates than those who feel otherwise.

 Clear and achievable expectations, with tools that fit the task, are critical for mental health.

In general, young people feel schools are good at expectation alignment.

Young people who agree or strongly agree with the following statements:

70%
Given my goals for the future, my school provides me with the tools I need to be successful.

69%
For the most part, my teachers/professors tell me what they expect of me and then help me succeed.

But there is room for improvement when it comes to what success looks like at school and who feels they can achieve that expectation.

Young people who agree or strongly agree with the following statements:

66%
Success at school is just about grades.

68%
Only certain types of students can really thrive at school.

S **THE SPRINGTIDE SERIES ON MENTAL HEALTH**

SPRINGTIDE KEY FINDINGS

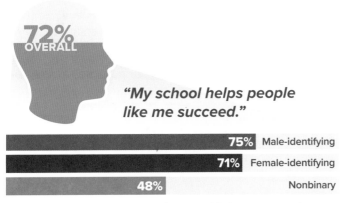

72% OVERALL

"My school helps people like me succeed."

75%	Male-identifying
71%	Female-identifying
48%	Nonbinary

Young people who agree or strongly agree with the statement above

Despite the high rate of mental-health concerns among young people ages 13 to 25, many don't turn to the resources schools provide.

This is a clear instance of a gap in expectation alignment. Schools promote the expectation that caring for mental health is important. They have tools, like full-time staff members or other resources, to help meet that expectation. But there are still gaps. Why?

We asked young people: *If you wanted to talk to a school counselor, school therapist, or school psychologist about emotional challenges or problems (not including career services, college prep, class scheduling, etc.) but didn't, what made you hesitate?*

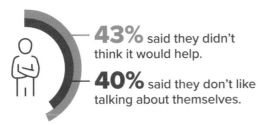

43% said they didn't think it would help.

40% said they don't like talking about themselves.

"There's a lot of pressure. I guess it's more like the pressure of expectations in my experience. I mean, you know, expect you to do well. If you're a student, the university expects you to do certain things and act a certain way as a student."

—Alia, 21

Mental Health & Gen Z
PURPOSE

A focus on fostering purpose on both an institutional and an individual level, versus reacting to mental-health concerns when they arise, can help promote mental healthiness among students. Students who agree that school is a place that helps them discover their purpose say they are "flourishing a lot" in their mental health at higher rates than those who feel otherwise.

 In general, students think school is a place to find their purpose.

Overall, the majority of students (65%) agree that "school is a place where I can ask questions and explore so that I can find my purpose in life." But nonbinary students are less likely to feel this way than their peers.

65% OVERALL

"School is a place where I can ask questions and explore so that I can find my purpose in life."

67%	Female-identifying
64%	Male-identifying
55%	Nonbinary

Young people who agree or strongly agree with the statement above

Young people who agree or strongly agree with the following statements:

60%
My school helps me figure out what I'm passionate about.

66%
I feel like school is just something I have to do, but it's not really connected to my purpose in the world.

THE SPRINGTIDE SERIES ON MENTAL HEALTH

SPRINGTIDE KEY FINDINGS

71%
of young people
say they are **religious**.

78%
of young people
say they are **spiritual**.

*While the majority of young people consider themselves religious (71%) or spiritual (78%), less than half of all students feel that their schools support or encourage this particular aspect of who they are and where they find a sense of purpose. **This is a missed opportunity for schools to engage.***

45% *of young people agree or strongly agree with the following statement:*

"My school, including instructors and staff, engage my faith/religion/spirituality in ways that help me discover my value and purpose in the world."

Purpose at school and the purpose of school are distinct. But they don't have to be.

Young people already assume that school itself has a certain purpose: to help them learn. And so there's a prevailing sense that their purpose at school is also singular: to get good grades. But fostering purpose at school also means encouraging young people to find their connection to something bigger than themselves.

"... She actually validated my experiences. She was like, *Oh, thank you for telling me this, and* [she said] *these are ways we can help you.* She directed me to some mental health resources."

—Kim, 18

CONNECTION AT SCHOOL
How to Create Belonging

"You feel the **connection with the teacher;** you know, if you really like the teacher and you know they like you back. You just know if it's comfortable; you know if you're able to let them know about [an] issue. . . you can **talk about life and about real world** problems and stuff, the kind of things that makes you more comfortable with the teacher. **They talk about that [kind of deep or real] stuff** on top of whatever they have to teach you."

—Cole, 16

"I was telling her how one of my family relatives passed away because of COVID, and while I was telling her this, I just started crying. But then **she actually validated my experiences**. She was like, *Oh, thank you for telling me this,* and [she said,] *these are ways we can help you.* She directed me to some mental health resources, and she sent an email to the university counseling center to ask for scheduling appointment availability."

—Kim, 18

"It's the ability to be able to say, *Hey, can I step out for a sec?* Because for example, when you hear this, you know, you think, *Hey, yeah, those students are just going to leave.* But nobody with her has taken advantage of that. They just step out of the classroom for a couple of minutes and they're like, *Okay, we're good. I'm going back in*. And it's because first of all, they treated with respect. Second, it's a welcoming space to everyone. And third, it's an open topic that she is willing to talk about with us."

—JJ, 15

Young people often say that talking about their mental-health problems with others helps them cope. Our *State of Religion & Young People, 2021: Navigating Uncertainty* report found that most young people ages 13 to 25 (55%) want someone who will listen—not advise or fix—when they're going through something difficult. And when it comes to the challenges of their mental health, young people don't share with just anyone. They want to talk to people they trust. The interview quotes on the previous page show that teachers can be pillars of trust for young people amid mental-health concerns. The 80 young people interviewed for this report linked their sense of trust to a variety of factors. They said trust might come from knowing someone for a long time, from having their experiences validated and needs supported, from the sense of mutual exchange and respect, and more.

Cole notes that he can trust his teacher because she makes it possible to talk about anything, rather than what's on the syllabus for the day. Kim describes the powerful experience of having a teacher validate her grief and then connect her to resources. JJ points out the mutual respect their teacher seems to have, trusting her students to take time they need without abusing the privilege of coming and going. In response to feeling respected, her students return to her classroom because they respect her.

Relational Authority is a framework for building trust, first introduced in *The State of Religion & Young People, 2020: Relational Authority*. Many of the themes that arose around trust in our interviews for this report, like those with Cole, Kim, and JJ, echo the principles we lay out in that framework, including the need for listening, integrity, transparency, care, and expertise. The whole report on Relational Authority is available online.

> **Young people who have more, and more significant, connections are less likely to suffer from mental illness.**

What is connection?

Connection describes the depth, number, and type of relationships a person has. Young people can be connected to one another, their families, friends, non-family adults, and even larger communities or groups. Schools are natural hubs of potential belonging, in both the large community of a whole school and the individual subcommunities that make it up. In this way, young people have the opportunity to forge relationships that can meet a variety of needs: numerous acquaintances with a few close connections, friendships or mentorships based on shared interests, and an overall sense of being connected to a whole "body" of other students, faculty, and staff. Because connection is not just about *gathering*, all these types of relationships are important within the school context.

Why does connection matter for mental health?

Young people who have more, and more significant, connections are less likely to suffer from mental illness. To say it another way, young people are more likely to report mental wellness and flourishing if they have relationships with friends, family members, and others. Sociologists sometimes refer to this sense of connection as social integration. The social sciences have demonstrated, in the words of sociologist Allan V. Horwitz, that "people with more frequent contacts with family, friends, and neighbors and who are involved with voluntary organizations such as churches, civic organizations, and clubs report better mental health than those who are more isolated."

Students who feel they belong at school say they are "flourishing a lot" in their mental health at higher rates than those who do not feel they belong.

⬤ Not flourishing ⬤ Flourishing a lot

I am lonely at school most of the time and do not want to be there most days.

57%

12%

I am lonely at school often, but there are still reasons to be at this school.

40%

15%

I am not lonely at school, but I also don't feel like I belong.

27%

24%

I sometimes feel like I belong at school, but it's not enough to feel secure.

27%

25%

I belong at school, and I feel like people know who I am.

15%

43%

Our data show that teachers have a role in students' feelings of belonging. Young people who say they have a meaningful interaction with a teacher or professor in a typical week report lower rates of loneliness, compared to those who do not have such interactions in a typical week. Eighty-seven percent of those who did not have a meaningful interaction with a teacher or professor said they are lonely at school most of the time and do not want to be there, compared to only 13% who had a meaningful interaction.

"I feel lonely at school most of the time and do not want to be there most days."

⬤ Had a meaningful interaction with a teacher or professor
⬤ Did **not** have a meaningful interaction with a teacher or professor

13%

87%

While we don't underestimate the critical role of administrators and other educational leaders, the touchpoint that teachers have in the lives of students cannot be overstated when it comes to connection. Still, *any* trusted adult at school can make a difference:

28% of people who say they do have at least one trusted adult at school also say they feel like they belong at school and people know who they are.

Only 15% of those who say they *do not* have at least one trusted adult say they feel like they belong at school and people know who they are.

Even without scientific studies, many people understand the importance of social connections for mental health. Natalia, a 22-year-old young woman interviewed for this report, captured what many of her peers indicated in both surveys and interviews about the importance of deep connection: "Community gives you the sense of not being so alone [even] in times that it apparently looks alone, like [when] there's no one around or my parents aren't here. In that aspect, [my community] reminds me that I belong somewhere with these people who understand me and have seen me grow up." She describes how feeling that she *belongs* to a group or community, even when she is alone, yields a positive experience of support for her.

A difficulty that many young people articulated in interviews is that isolation is both a *cause* of mental unwellness and a *response* to it. While Mason, 21, understands the value of a supportive community, he also notices the urge to retreat into isolation, almost as a defense mechanism. "The part of mental health that can be difficult is that sometimes people kind of **cave in** and corner themselves and isolate themselves from other people. And I think that can be very dangerous because when they do that, they may be in a state where they can't properly help themselves . . . but then there's no one there to tell them like, *Hey, this is not good for you.*"

Mason notes the temptation to turn inward when struggling but also why connection is so important for mental health: to have someone notice something is wrong. Sociologists point to this when confirming that being connected (or "socially integrated") has positive consequences for mental health: because *being noticed* matters.

Springtide has long had an interest in how Gen Z experiences belonging. Our data show that 62% of young people with *no trusted adults* agree with the statement "I feel completely alone," and only 9% of young people with five or more trusted adults in their lives agree with the same statement. In other words, trusted adults are a critical piece for helping young people experience belonging.

Facilitating connection for young people in schools is one of the first steps to becoming an organization that is mental-health friendly. How can educational leaders foster connections that help young people feel they belong?

How to Create Belonging

Young people's experiences of belonging must be cultivated by trusted adults. And belonging deepens through an identifiable process. In 2020, Springtide released a report titled *Belonging: Reconnecting America's Loneliest Generation*, which demonstrated a pattern in the stories of young people as they moved from initial joining to experiences of belonging. Three distinct feelings kept surfacing as they talked: feeling noticed, being named, and feeling known. This pattern also surfaced in the interviews we conducted for this report. We refer to this pattern of moving from *noticed* to *named* to *known* as the **Belongingness Process**.

Young people initially enter relationships, groups, and organizations because of certain commonalities—shared interests, values, beliefs, practices, vocations, or professions. But they stay in those relationships when they feel like they belong.

Schools appear ripe with potential for connections—connections among peers and with teachers, mentors, coaches, and more. However, most students aren't connected in ways that matter for mental well-being. Only 20% of students tell us they feel they belong at their school and feel people know who they are. Almost two-thirds (63%) say they don't even *sometimes* feel like they belong or feel known. So, while a sense of connection in schools is often possible, it doesn't always happen.

Only 20% of students tell us **they feel they belong at their school and feel people know who they are**.

Almost two-thirds (63%) say **they don't even sometimes feel like they belong or feel known**.

The Belongingness Process

Springtide's Belongingness Process identifies three steps or building blocks for creating belonging for young people. And this experience of belonging—of deep and varied connections within a community—is critical for their mental health at school. For each step, trusted adults can take obvious actions. Schools often do well with these critical building blocks, but there are opportunities to dig deeper into each of these dimensions as well, to increase belonging in educational settings.

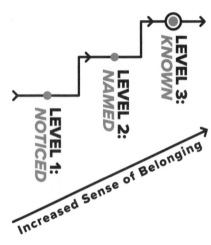

LEVEL 1: (I am) Noticed

The perception of being noticed by another—being seen or acknowledged, even in the most straightforward ways—is the initial step toward a sense of belonging. It is here that young people describe the power of being invited into relationship and having others become interested in them. Consider this comment from a young person we interviewed when conducting our initial research for *Belonging*: "The dominant experience of young people when it comes to interacting with adults is of being dismissed. I just don't expect them to pay attention to me." The simple act of seeing generates an initial sense of belongingness for a young person, which creates a foundation for deeper relationships.

We asked young people to tell us whether they experience being *noticed* at school. The majority of young people do feel they are acknowledged by adults or peers on a daily basis while at school.

71% Adults **acknowledge my presence at my school**.

78% At my school, **at least one person says hello to me every day**.

While most students agree that they don't feel they need to hide who they are at school (63%) or confirm that they don't feel anonymous or invisible at school (61%), the margins for those who don't agree are significant. This opportunity to "notice" students at a deeper level, to see the students who are marginalized and make a special effort to connect with them, is critical for building a community of belonging.

63% of students agree with the statement *"I don't feel I need to hide who I am at my school."*

61% of students agree with the statement *"I do not feel anonymous or invisible at my school."*

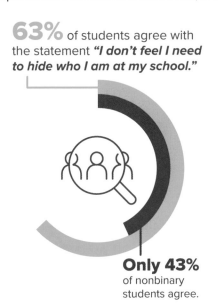

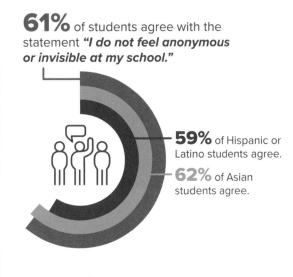

59% of Hispanic or Latino students agree.

62% of Asian students agree.

Only 43% of nonbinary students agree.

Tide-Turning Tip

Help facilitate peer-to-peer connections. When it comes to conversations about mental health, young people naturally turn to one another. Therefore, the more peer connections they have, the better. You can facilitate these connections by providing opportunities for students to build community. And you can help young people *help one another* not only with more connections but with more skills. Consider extending mental-health first-aid and awareness training to students so they can be better equipped to help their friends and, importantly, so they know when to bring a concern to a trusted adult. Sports teams, dorm communities, music groups, book clubs—all these types of communities can be strengthened with more opportunities to connect *outside* the primary activity (that is, by hosting retreats or dining nights together), and with more opportunities to learn how to care for one another well.

LEVEL 2: (I am) Named

The use of a person's name or correct pronoun triggers an immediate connection. It demonstrates a commitment to their participation in the classroom or school; it builds on *noticing* and makes a young person feel a deeper sense of being connected. Psychologists and linguists confirm that naming someone elevates them in importance and status. In many ways, our name forms and shapes our identity, and using someone's name confirms that you are in a relationship with them.

We asked young people whether they experience being *named* at school. Schools are doing well helping young people, in general, experience being named. About three out of four students say that adults at their school remember their name and greet them by it (or another personal way) at school.

77% Adults at my school remember my name.

73% Adults greet me by name or in some other personal way at my school.

Tide-Turning Tip

Use students' preferred names and make a point of pronouncing them correctly from day one. Educators know the importance of learning their students' names, which is often a priority in those first few weeks of a new class. We'd like to encourage you to learn your students' names before they step foot in your classroom. Make a point of asking all students their preferred name and personal pronouns as a part of school registration, and make sure these names are on all school rosters so that from the first

But to be named extends beyond identifying someone correctly. Naming someone also refers to the relational aspect mentioned above. Educators can strengthen the good work they are already doing in this area. Only about half (56%) of young people agree with the statement "Adults at my school miss me when I have not been in school for some reason." When we look at young people who feel otherwise—young people who *disagree* that adults at their school miss their presence when they are absent—it's middle schoolers and public college students who are most likely to feel anonymous.

Young people who *disagree* or *strongly disagree* with the statement below:

"Adults at my school miss me when I have not been in school for some reason."

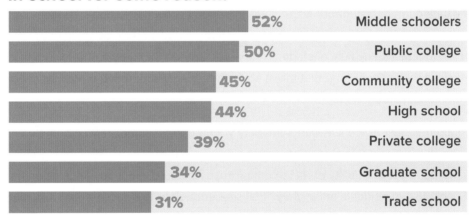

52%	Middle schoolers
50%	Public college
45%	Community college
44%	High school
39%	Private college
34%	Graduate school
31%	Trade school

Because our samples of each population are small, they are indicative—though not conclusive—about which students might feel they are "unnamed" in the context of school.

day of school all students can be literally named. Likewise, before taking attendance, be sure you know how to pronounce each student's name correctly. Properly greeting each student starts that very basic connection of saying that you care. If teaching a large lecture where learning everyone's name isn't possible, consider ways to help students learn *one another's* names early on in the semester with opening questions that prompt conversation between and among different students.

LEVEL 3: KNOWN

LEVEL 3: (I am) Known

Belongingness reaches a new level when a person feels known. This depth of belongingness, this sense of *feeling known*, builds on being noticed and named but adds the all-important dimension of unreserved acceptance. Freed from the fear of rejection, young people feel safe having open, honest conversations. They are more likely to share hopes, anxieties, challenges, and joys alike. In essence, they experience trust within that relationship. This kind of acceptance has immeasurable significance as an antidote for loneliness, isolation, and stress. Accepting young people without judgment is an essential condition for deep belongingness.

We asked young people whether they experience being *known* at school. Once again, the data capturing student perspectives in general show that schools are doing a good job encouraging safety and not being judgmental, thus creating an environment of belonging. Nearly 70% of students surveyed agreed that they feel safe with most adults at their schools and that those adults are openly supportive as well as curious without being judgmental.

Importantly, just as we see with nonbinary young people in the statistic on the next page, this *general* sense of safety within relationships at school does not always translate to the possibility of real depth or trust. As noted in our key findings on page 18, only 18% of students tell us they "feel safe enough to talk about what really matters to me" at school. For Black or African American students, this figure drops to 11%.

Tide-Turning Tip

Look for outliers. Consider students who are likely to *not* feel they are a part of your school community—transfer students, students who do not have resources to participate in extracurricular activities, students whose families cannot easily access communications provided by the school because of language barriers or technological gaps, students with external interests not recognized by the school, and so on. Assess

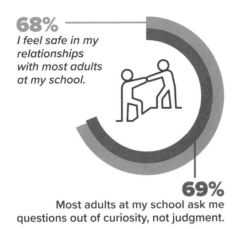

68%
I feel safe in my relationships with most adults at my school.

69%
Most adults at my school ask me questions out of curiosity, not judgment.

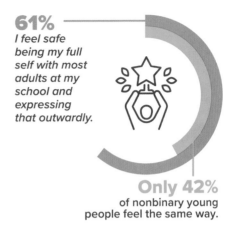

61%
I feel safe being my full self with most adults at my school and expressing that outwardly.

Only 42%
of nonbinary young people feel the same way.

68%
OVERALL

"Most adults at my school are openly supportive of me."

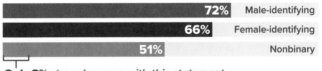

72%	Male-identifying
66%	Female-identifying
51%	Nonbinary

***Only 8%** strongly agree with this statement.*

● ● ●

Schools are doing a good job helping students feel *noticed*, *named*, and *known* on a basic level. However, there are important places where educators can strive to dig deeper into this dynamic and truly create a sense of belonging that leads to connection. Taking action dedicated to building connection in schools is a sure way to create an environment that is mental-health friendly at its very core.

what you do to help these students, and what you don't do. How might you help them? To help generate some ideas, Springtide has created a free 6-week email series, *The Belongingness Challenge,* that sends a weekly prompt to help you integrate practices of belonging into your everyday work with young people. If you are interested, learn more and sign up here. *springtideresearch.org/belongingness-challenge*

A CLOSER LOOK
REDESIGNING OUR SOCIAL STRUCTURES

I teach an introduction to developmental psychology course at an elite institution. During my first few terms, I noticed the number of students dropping the course after the first exam if they did not achieve a near-perfect score. I saw how stressed students became if their grades threatened to drop below 90%. I tried to comfort and reassure them, but the outcomes were the same. Highly capable students were stressed, anxious, and dropping the course. This was not because they didn't enjoy the content, but because they needed to maintain a high GPA. I became curious about this pervasive pattern of stress and anxiety and about what I could do, in my class, to change the learning climate.

From my research on how young people develop their identity, and in particular how those in the United States learn to thrive, I know that mental health is not (solely) a problem of individuals. It is a problem with roots in our social structures and thus requires structural solutions.

This is precisely what this Springtide report calls attention to: If we want to support the mental health and thriving of young people, we have to reimagine core values and metrics of success in this society—in our institutions, our classrooms, our communities, and our homes.

The United States is a society designed from its inception for some to get ahead and for others to fall (and stay) behind. Those with power enslaved people, stole land, and annihilated cultures, and we now live in a society where racism, sexism, and patriarchy are woven into the very fabric of US social structures. The country's capitalistic values favor individualism, commodification, productivity, and profit. Neither US society nor its institutions—including schools—were built for *all people* to thrive.

The social sciences show that human beings need genuine connection with others, the experience of meeting achievable expectations, and a sense of purpose and meaning in life. The social sciences also show that the cultural values that have grounded the United States for centuries (individualism, competition, dominance and power, monetary success, etc.) are not only incompatible with cooperation, kindness, moral justice, and equality but that such values undermine the core needs and desires of human beings.

Though exacerbated by the COVID-19 pandemic, a resurgence of anti-Black and anti-Asian racism, and an uptick in explicit white supremacist violence, the mental-health crisis is not surprising. Our survival as human beings depends not on the mechanisms of individual self-care but on empathy and caring relationships.

A CLOSER LOOK

> If we want to support the mental health and thriving of young people, we have to reimagine core values and metrics of success in this society—in our institutions, our classrooms, our communities, and our homes.
>
> —Dr. Onnie Rogers

When I assessed what I saw happening with the students in my course, rather than focus on individual students who were stressed and anxious (and there were plenty of them!), I evaluated the structure of my course and whether my classroom was cultivating community, engagement, and meaningful learning. I asked myself several questions: Does the structure of this course cultivate curiosity and belonging? Does it provide the tools needed for all or many to succeed? Does it connect with young people's natural eagerness to explore and ask questions? Or does it nurture individualism, competition, and performance?

I found that despite my intention for students to critically engage with the course material and apply it to their lived experiences and their own questions, the *structure* of my lectures and exams emphasized individual knowledge, performance, and competition. This left little space for students to build meaningful connections, engage curiosity, or make novel discoveries.

In restructuring my course, I aimed to cultivate a learning space centered on relationships, curiosity, equity, and discovery. I replaced all exams with applied assignments where students use developmental theory for tasks such as evaluating infant toys and critiquing children's media. I opened space for students to choose topics and conduct their own research.

The difference was transformational. The students are more engaged and less anxious. They are no longer dropping the course—and their work is exceptional. They report how much they appreciate a learning space where they are encouraged and free to think, explore, ask questions, and genuinely learn. I changed the structure, and student stress and anxiety plummeted while learning soared. Offering study sessions and tea and cookies, or dog-petting as Lana describes on pages 10–11, may help students *survive* in an oppressive context, but changing the context made space for them to *thrive*. This is what it means to transform institutions to support mental health.

Dr. Onnie Rogers *is a developmental psychologist and assistant professor of psychology and education at Northwestern University. Dr. Rogers teaches courses on social and emotional development and understanding research through a lens of equity and justice. She also conducts research on youth identity development with a focus on the ways young people make sense of and resist social inequalities and stereotypes related to race, gender, and social class. Additionally, Dr. Rogers directs the Development of Identities in Cultural Environments (DICE) research lab, where she mentors undergraduate and graduate students in research. Married during college, Dr. Rogers and her husband have 17 years of partnership and two young daughters.*

A CLOSER LOOK

EXPECTATIONS AT SCHOOL
How to Create Expectation and Tool Alignment

"I have friends who are **punished if they don't get As**. And I think it **puts a lot of stress on them, especially when** they're already going through problems that are not recognized by their parents. I think there is a lot of pressure put on us to do really well, to balance all of these things, you know, especially when our mental health concerns are not being heard, it makes it even harder."

—Ara, 16

"The stereotype is that [mental health] is a freedom from all forms of anxiety or whatever. I mean, if you have no anxiety in your life, you're probably dead. So I think it's important that you just are able to **manage** your anxiety or the normal stresses of day-to-day life."

— Spencer, 22

"They'll say, you know, *Hey, you hear mental health matters to us,* but then there's very little action to be taken because how can you act? **How are you going to tell me that my mental health matters when I'm staying up all night, I'm pulling all-nighters to get an A in this class?** And then in the same breath, say like, *Oh, growth mindset.* [. . .] It's like, **you're telling me two completely different things. You're telling me that I need an A**, that I need to succeed. I need to be the best. It's so competitive. **And then you're [also] telling me that my mental health matters**. . . . It seems very like optic . . . yeah, it's performative."

—Araceli, 25

"Even your guidance counselors at school will be like, *Oh, is everything okay? Oh no, it's not? Well,* **I'll help you, but you have to get a good grade on your test because you don't want your grades suffering**. It's stuff like that. Like . . . we just need somebody to talk to, who's going to help us. Who doesn't have any motive besides just wanting us to get better. . . . Our guidance counselors, even though they're great, they have that mode of like, *Okay,* **how are we going to pass those classes?** *And how are we going to make you feel better about life?"*

—Julie, 17

Young people like Ara, Araceli, Spencer, and Julie voice something we hear consistently during interviews: Students are overwhelmed. They feel immense pressure. When asked how school impacts their mental health, nearly every young person we interviewed described stress, pressure, anxiety, and burnout. Ara describes the way pressure *about* school doesn't just come from school, but from several sources. Julie and Araceli express frustration when those who are *supposed* to equip them to succeed offer only check-ins that double-down on the importance of fulfilling the expectations already in place. Spencer notes that he doesn't expect total relief from anxiety, but just the ability to *manage* it, the chance to not be totally overwhelmed by day-to-day expectations.

What is expectation?

Expectations are standards that emerge from narratives about how to succeed in life. Young people experience varied and layered sets of expectations. Springtide's interest in expectations is not just that social narratives exist about who and how to be in the world but also how those expectations *are* or *are not* realistically achievable for young people at school.

Making expectations achievable for students is a matter of aligning expectations and tools to make sure students are prepared to succeed. Alignment is about making sure the tools fit the task, and vice versa. And schools are at the forefront of a movement toward better reconciliation between student needs and classroom expectations. Our data demonstrate that the majority of young people *do* feel they have the tools they need to succeed at school. As mentioned on page 20 of this report, 70% of young people in school today agree that "given my goals for the future, my school provides me with the tools I need to be successful." Nearly the same percentage (69%) tell us that "for the most part, my teachers/professors tell me what they expect of me and then help me succeed." Sixty-seven percent of all young people currently in school tell us that "I understand who the people in charge of my school are, and I know who to go to for what I need." So, the first step in creating alignment is to *keep doing what you're doing*, especially when it comes to academic expectations about success at school.

Why does expectation alignment matter for mental health?

This alignment between expectations and tools has a critical impact on young people's mental health. **We know that students who strongly agree they have the tools they need for success are "flourishing a lot" in their mental health at higher rates than those who feel strongly otherwise.**

Young people who agree that *"given my goals for the future, my school provides me with the tools I need to be successful"* are more likely to say they are *"flourishing a lot in my mental health"* than those who disagree.

● Agree   ● Disagree

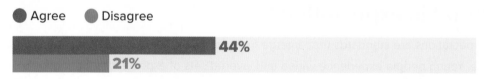

44%

21%

Imagine, for a moment, that every day a young person wakes up, heads to school, and is asked to help grow a community garden. But they're given half-empty watering cans and plastic spoons instead of shovels. No matter how good the instructors, how valuable the lesson, or how impassioned that young person is about gardening, these tools cannot sustain the activity. Frustration is inevitable. Additionally, if a young person internalizes the sense that *others* are making these tools work, or if educators insist that the work is manageable, the young person will begin to see the poor tools as a reflection of their own capability.

A sense of frustration and almost *defeat* is palpable in our conversation with Grace, a ninth grader interviewed in the context of a classroom focus group. She explains the ways competing or unclear expectations show up with regularity in schools:

> " . . . It's hard because expectations are always changing based on who you go to. So one teacher might expect everything of you and another one might not care as much. Or the way that they teach might change between teachers. And that's fine, I totally understand that everyone is different, but then they teach you how to [do something basic like] write paragraphs differently, and then everything that you are used to [and already learned] completely vanishes. . . . Their grading system is different, and everything just changes."
>
> —Grace

If a school makes it clear that success means good grades, but each teacher or professor requires vastly different or even competing routes about how that success is to be accomplished, young people's mental health suffers. Grace continues: "People with power are able to change things, and people without power, kinda like us, can't change things, and that can affect your mental health because it feels like you can't do anything about it." If, as Julia notes in her interview, a guidance counselor appears available to help ease mental health burdens but only serves to reinforce expectations that feel unattainable or overwhelming to students, students' mental health suffers.

Rosaline, a ninth grader from the same focus group during which we spoke with Grace, echoes what many of our interviewees tell us: that tasks that make you "think you aren't good enough to do something" hurt their mental health. Replacing the plastic spoon with a shovel or filling the watering cans empowers Rosaline and her peers to succeed but also helps them internalize a healthier assessment of their skills and worth.

Sociological research shows that organizations that provide clear, consistent expectations—about what it takes to be a good student, how to write a paragraph properly, and everything in between—can help bolster mental health. Otherwise, like Grace and Rosaline articulate, the lack of clarity or consistency is internalized personally. Helping young people meet expectations (even high expectations) is a matter of aligning the right tools with these clear, consistent expectations.

How to Create Expectation Alignment

How can educational leaders help foster healthy expectations? By building on strengths already at work and by evaluating the gaps in these efforts. Any gaps between what's expected and what's perceived as achievable can help leaders determine what to pay attention to when it comes to creating a positive mental-health environment for young people.

Build on What's Working

Recall, as noted in the introduction to this report, that 70% of young people in school today agree that "given my goals for the future, my school provides me with the tools I need to be successful." And almost the same number of students (69%) tell us that "for the most part, my teachers/professors tell me what they expect of me and then help me succeed." Young people are overwhelmed by school, but the majority also tell us they have the tools and support to succeed.

We asked young people to tell us whether it was true, in their experience, that "my school helps people *like me* succeed." A positive sign is that young people of various racial and ethnic backgrounds respond affirmatively at about the same rate to this statement.

Young people who *agree* or *strongly agree* with the statement below:
"My school helps people like me succeed," by race.

Asian

76%

Black or African American

74%

Hispanic or Latino

72%

White

70%

This is great news—young people of different races feel that their school helps *students like them* succeed. There are expectations for success, and the majority of students feel like the tools offered in service of that expectation are available to them, specifically.

A movement over the past 10 to 15 years toward a more student-centered school environment is no doubt at the heart of this kind of strong expectation alignment. Teacher training, early responses to crisis (mental health and otherwise), and availability of resources (whether teachers, clubs, or concrete tools) designed to help young people of all races succeed are positive and conscientious shifts rooted in evaluating the real and diverse needs of this generation. Schools that have adopted practices that consider the needs of young people help create alignment because young people are not responsible for closing the gap on unachievable expectations. Schools don't necessarily do this by lowering expectations, but by adjusting them or refining the tools.

Here's an example of an expectation that remains high but is made more achievable with a refined tool. Students are expected to get good grades. A growing body of research emphasizes the importance of sleep for adolescent development. In order to improve alignment between the expectation (to do well at school) and the tool that helps young people meet it, many schools have adopted later start times. Beginning classes later aligns with teens' biological rhythms but doesn't compromise the length of a school day or the amount of work a student is expected to do.

Tide-Turning Tip

Celebrate. Students can find it hard to see how small successes build toward a bigger goal, especially when the path toward a goal requires many steps. Celebrating the actions that students take to move toward their goals can help them see how their actions fill the gap between where they are and where they want to be. And by celebrating the completion of small steps toward a bigger goal, you help orient students who may otherwise feel unmotivated by what they perceive to be busywork or tasks unrelated to their goals.

Evaluate the Gaps

Efforts toward student-centered classrooms and school policies—like later start times or even pedagogy inclusive of different learning styles—have been happening in educational spaces for a decade or longer in many places. But these efforts are not necessarily happening *evenly*. Expectations are clearly *misaligned* in some places. More than 2 out of 3 (68%) young people tell us that "only certain types of students can really thrive here," referring to their schools. Perhaps those "certain types" are perceived to be the academically inclined. Perhaps they are the wealthy, who have resources to pay for tutoring or, at the very least, don't have to get an after-school job that competes with time otherwise spent on homework or extracurricular activities.

Our data show that one population feeling left behind in the success narratives are nonbinary young people. Fewer than half of nonbinary students agree with the statement "My school helps people like me succeed." By comparison, 75% of males and 71% of females say their schools help people like them succeed.

Young people who *agree* or *strongly agree* with the statement:

"My school helps people like me succeed," by gender.

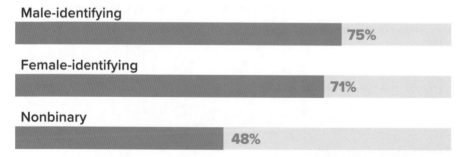

Male-identifying

75%

Female-identifying

71%

Nonbinary

48%

The students in your educational environment who feel the reverse—that their school *does not* help people like them succeed—may or may not mirror the 25% of males, 29% of females, and 52% of nonbinary young people we surveyed. But it's important to know who these students are in your context and to identify the gaps. Why do they feel they are not equipped with the tools to find success at school?

The missed opportunity, as well as the toll on mental health, of misalignment between expectations and tools is evident when we ask young people about accessing mental-health services at school. And one of the places where the tools don't always match expectations pertains to mental-health services explicitly.

We asked young people: If you wanted to talk to a school counselor, school therapist, or school psychologist about emotional challenges or problems (not including career services, college prep, class scheduling, etc.), but *didn't do so*, what made you hesitate?

What made you hesitate to get help?

(Young people could select more than one answer.)

I didn't have time.
27%

I didn't think my issues were big enough to bother someone with.
31%

I felt like I would be judged.
33%

I don't like talking about myself.
40%

I didn't think it would help.
43%

Very few mentioned financial (11%) or scheduling (7%) hurdles, and only 11% said they don't think therapy is useful for emotional and mental health. All of this confirms that the emphasis schools place on the expectation (i.e., that by having therapy as a resource, there is at least an implicit message that therapy is good and helpful for mental health) is clearly understood, and that the tools for meeting that expectation (i.e., the availability, affordability, and logistics of meeting with a mental-health professional) are in sync. Students know that their mental health matters, and they know who to turn to and how if they are in need.

But still, many young people, including those who may need it, do not take advantage of the mental-health services at their schools. Asking them *why* tells us about gaps that are not yet accounted for in this process of aligning expectations and tools.

Young people may have clear ideas about what it takes to succeed at school, and they may even have access to the things and people that will *help* them succeed. For schools, the breakdown in expectation and tool alignment may be that certain types of students do not feel that the tools are designed to help *them*, specifically. Other gaps may not be about unclear expectations or poor tools, but some subtler reasons students don't feel able to take advantage of the tools themselves.

Our data suggest that major structural changes that fundamentally reinvent the educational system are not needed to keep up the good work already underway when it comes to better alignment around expectations and tools at school. Instead, there are ways to better foster this alignment where gaps still exist. A lack of alignment between expectations and tools can be harmful for young people's mental health. Inversely, *achievable expectations that foster growth* are beneficial to have in place in any organization. Young people want to be pushed and challenged. They don't want to be defeated, and they don't want to be discouraged.

Tide-Turning Tip

Take advantage of the years. Students consistently tell us that they feel comfortable talking to adults they trust, and that one of the key factors in building trust is time. Consider assigning an adult mentor to all students for their entire time with your institution. Be it a counselor or adviser or homeroom teacher, this adult can be someone students can connect with beyond the purpose of grades—ideally, this mentor is *not* a teacher who is in a position to assign a grade to students. These mentors don't need to be trained mental-health practitioners, but they should be open to listening and willing to help a student find the resources they need.

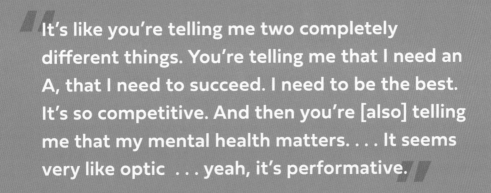

"It's like you're telling me two completely different things. You're telling me that I need an A, that I need to succeed. I need to be the best. It's so competitive. And then you're [also] telling me that my mental health matters. . . . It seems very like optic . . . yeah, it's performative."

—Araceli, 25

A CLOSER LOOK
YOUNG PEOPLE REFLECT ON CONNECTION, EXPECTATION, AND PURPOSE

We asked our Springtide Ambassadors, a group of young people who meet monthly to discuss Springtide data and themes, to contribute a piece of writing for this report, reflecting on the concepts of connection, expectation, and purpose at school.

This contribution was edited by Springtide Ambassador Daniel.

CONNECTION . . . *from Blake, Abby, and Lauren*

A lack of a genuine connection between students, teachers, and administrators truly affects the well-being of the student body. Understandably, schools have to focus on curriculum development and setting up students for success on things like standardized tests. But this focus gives us the impression that our worth at school is contingent on achievement. And because funding is contingent on our achievement, it can feel really transactional—the opposite of connection.

Our sense is that in many school environments, the staff and administration promote that they "care" about students and their mental health. Our schools have resources for teens to use in situations when mental-health issues arise, but creating an open, proactive environment supportive of students' mental health has to be the goal.

Educators need to know how crucial it is to empathize with students and to really connect with us on more than the schoolwork. As students, we appreciate when we can confide in teachers when we're struggling or behind. It's not just that we need less pressure from school sometimes. It's that we need more grace, more understanding, from those we're connected to at school too.

EXPECTATION . . . *from Grace, Peyton, and Eva*

"What are you gonna be when you grow up?" "Make sure your grades are perfect." "Make sure you're doing every club and sport that you can." We hear these narratives and expectations regularly. By the age of 14, we feel pressured to know what career path we will take, to participate in multiple extracurricular activities, and to excel academically, all while making sure to have fun since we're still young. Schools define success by slim margins of intelligence and accomplishment. Our self-worth falls into that same slim margin of what's acceptable.

A student could get five As and one B, and, whether intentional or not, it seems the one slightly lower grade gets all the attention. Schools don't need to add to the pressure students already put on themselves about what it means to succeed. Our mental health is at an all-time low. We need help to feel better. We don't need a conversation about why we got a B instead of an A.

It's almost like a "workaholic" expectation has entered our schooling system. Young people feel shame when taking breaks unless in a crisis. But we don't want to have to hit rock bottom to take a break and a deep breath.

PURPOSE . . . *from Sophie, Sofia, and Acadia*

Most high school students are never encouraged to pursue anything that isn't directly related to college ambitions. We are expected to do clubs, sports, AP classes, college classes, and work, all so that we can get into a good college. But what is the purpose of all this? It seems that our understanding of our purpose in life—something that ought to be tied to our very humanity—is instead chained to the ways we can be useful, eventually, to society at large.

Schools seem to emphasize the pressure to achieve constant success and to be perpetually busy for the singular goal of college. This pressure, however, hinders students' opportunity to discover or pursue goals of their own and contributes to the day-to-day tedium of education.

Rarely does anyone explain why we're studying geometry or reading Shakespeare beyond the immediate goal—to pass a test or class. Rarely do we hear the ways we're worth more than the quantitative product of our labor. Rarely does our education at school feel designed to do more than produce workers with good resumes, rather than help us come alive.

At times it seems that schools' systems push the idea of college and career so much that they forget to tend to students' hearts and souls. We're in school systems for most of our childhood and young adult years. Although schools are not the only way we might discover our purpose, we spend the formative years of our lives here—schools should at least not hinder the ways we seek purpose, well-being, and mental health.

> **"Schools should at least not hinder the ways we seek purpose, well-being, and mental health."**

Participants in the Springtide Ambassadors Program (SAP) directly shape the research efforts and nationwide community engagement of Springtide Research Institute by participating in group collaboration and personal reflection. They meet monthly for more than a year with a steady, online cohort.

Ten ambassadors, spanning two cohorts, composed this reflection. Their voices represent seven states from different regions of the nation and public and private school experience. Their current ages range from 13 to 24. They hold various identities, including Black, Hispanic or Latino, Asian, multiracial, white, queer, straight, and more. Their diverse social locations and creeds inform their perspectives. We are proud to have their varied voices and ideas represented here and throughout our many Springtide resources.

PURPOSE AT SCHOOL

How to Create Mission

"I feel like we're at the age where we're experiencing a lot **and we're trying to decide how we feel about those experiences**."

— Misty, 17

"I think I'm nothing compared to a large body of water or a rainstorm. I'm really just a little person with little feelings in my little head and this world is in my little head. It, the world, is so much bigger than that, yet not. . . . I think the big thing for me, struggling with mental health for the past like 10 years of my life, maybe like 15 years, [is that] **I've learned to be comforted by the fact that . . . I'm so small, I'm so small. It makes me feel better. It makes me feel like if I make a mistake, it's really not as big of a deal as I thought it was**."

— Araceli, 25

"And for [the] meaning of life, I find my meaning of life to enjoy when you can. So I like to spend a lot of time doing the things I like to do: playing games, watching movies, talking with my friends. I don't particularly see myself as someone who has to have a specific goal or who finds myself being someone who has a life that's like, *Oh, I can't believe I'm not doing anything meaningful.* I mean, I find it fulfilling just to be happy."

— Paisley, 18

"When I look back at the times I felt overwhelmed, I step back and realize the things stressing me out were the same things that used to give me joy. And I realize why they shifted. Because [the pressure to] *maximize every minute of every hour* is not healthy, even though that's the societal message. The things that brought me joy just became another kind of pressure."

— Laura, 16

Young people ages 13 to 25 are in a period of life between childhood and adulthood. They are discovering their sense of purpose in life. Misty notes this time of exploration—experiencing life while also trying to make sense of it. Paisley summarizes what we heard from many young people in interviews for this report: that they are just beginning to land on certain core beliefs and values that help anchor and orient them, whether those values are family, the chance to turn inward, or prioritizing the pursuit of happiness over and above pressures to be wildly ambitious.

Laura, Araceli, and Paisley discuss how a sense of purpose has positively impacted their mental wellness. In each of these vignettes, and in many other interviews, we heard young people telling us how they adjusted and reframed an expectation, a pressure, or a cultural value to better match their own sense of purpose.

What is purpose?

Purpose is an aim that motivates a person. Cultivating purpose at school is about helping students develop a sense of what they want to accomplish, who they want to become, how they want to make a difference or move through the world. This means helping them connect to something bigger than themselves, something capable of giving direction to their days. This can be a subject they're passionate about, a community they're involved with, a spiritual practice that grounds them, a belief in a divine source, or more. In interviews, many young people mention their family or friends as the source of purpose in their lives. Others mention their faith or connection to a higher power. However, even religious and spiritual young people are unlikely to say that religious *spaces* help them discover their sense of meaning and purpose in life.

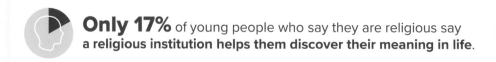

Only 17% of young people who say they are religious say **a religious institution helps them discover their meaning in life**.

As turning to religious institutions for conversations about meaning declines, young people nonetheless need spaces that help them discover a sense of purpose. Our data show that schools—with professionals who are trained and passionate about exposing young people to new ideas and possibilities—are central places for this critical work.

Why does purpose matter for mental health?

There is a strong and significant correlation between mental wellness and purpose, including the chance to seek purpose at school. And it's not just evident in our interviews for this report; our survey data confirm that **students who strongly agree school is a place that helps them discover their purpose are "flourishing a lot" in their mental health at higher rates than those who feel strongly otherwise.**

Young people who agree that *"school is a place where I can ask questions and explore so that I can find my purpose in life"* are more likely to say they are *"flourishing a lot in my mental health"* than those who disagree.

● Agree ● Disagree

46%

15%

Sociologists have shown that groups that prioritize the pursuit of meaning and purpose, both as a group and among individuals, have positive effects in mental wellness of their members. When this work is done on the individual level, it might be called purpose. When an organization has a sense of purpose—the kind that models and encourages individual exploration—it's called mission.

At schools, "mission" may feel like a closed question. Many young people feel that the goal of school is only to challenge young people academically (in fact, 66% of young people say the only way to succeed in school is to get good grades). But when teachers and other adults in educational settings help students see *why* what's being asked of them matters—a certain assignment or task or topic—young people can (and often do!) remark that they are more motivated about the task. Any task can shift from busywork to meaningful work. Like the young people quoted at the beginning of this chapter, this is another example of adjusting or reframing an expectation, a pressure, or a cultural value to better match and cohere with one's sense of purpose. In the social sciences, this is called **cognitive reframing**.

Our data provide lots of clues that young people are already doing this work on their own, even if they don't do it consistently or know what to call it. Araceli's sense of smallness, for example, didn't make her lose purpose but rather rooted her sense of purpose *beyond herself*. Laura discerned for herself the line between what she called "productive pressure" and pressure that made her want to give up on things: "Productive pressure is when I've got good energy and excitement about why I'm doing it." This distinction helped her figure out that she didn't need to give up the things she loved even when they added pressure to her life. Instead, she could adjust how she approached an activity, like ballet, so that her sense of purpose in that activity was better intact. Often, young people tell us that the difference between a pressure that overwhelms and one that stretches and causes growth is not just a matter of having the right tools but also having a sense of purpose in shouldering the pressure.

Schools that help young people discover their sense of purpose and help them see how that purpose connects to the school's overall mission can help mitigate mental-health concerns.

How to Create Mission

If a young person can be reminded that a certain subject, task, or course is *integrally connected to a larger goal*, they tell us over and over that this is the difference between pressure that burns them out and pressure that helps them grow. This is true whether *they've* set the goal or the goal has been set for them. Take Hayden, for example.

Hayden is 15 years old, a sophomore in high school. When asked where he finds purpose, he said that he finds it in "getting good grades in school because everyone likes getting good grades in school," and then added:

> "But I also play trombone, and I'm fairly good at it . . . It's really nice being able to go to like a performance or something and do really well and get all that praise. That's probably the most productive thing I do. And it's great. I love doing it. It's fun."

> —Hayden, 15

When asked more about why he feels this sense of purpose about playing trombone, he elaborated: "Well, like, [the band] wouldn't be the same without me. Because I'm the only person there who plays bass trombone. " This sense of purpose comes not only from playing a unique role in the band but also from being invited personally to consider the instrument. "The band director came up to me after school one day and was like, *Hey, I need a bass trombonist. You.* I went with it. It's a lot harder than the normal trombone, but I like it."

By making music with a group of his peers, Hayden is able to connect to something bigger than himself. The chance to *contribute* to his band in a unique way, as an individual, solidifies this sense of purpose. This common extracurricular became a purpose-filled activity for Hayden because of how it was framed: as an invitation to make a unique and needed contribution to a group. Laura's story is similar. A talented ballerina, Laura realized that her passion for ballet waned whenever she fell into thinking about it as just one of the many to-dos on her list of school and extracurricular demands. When she reframed that thinking to recall why she loved ballet in the first place—as an escape from the noisiness of other tasks, a chance to move her body, do art, and be with friends—she rediscovered her sense of purpose.

Jack, a 22-year-old young professional who entered the teaching profession working with special-needs students immediately after college, helpfully connects why this method of reframing can work for both students *and* educators in the context of school. When he thinks of the pressure and anxiety that come from school, he is thinking of the pressure he feels as a teacher.

> "The expectations in this job are consistently high; the demands can be intense. I started with a lot of passion but am already feeling how easily burnout happens. How do I rekindle that sense of purpose that first motivated me? Lately, I try reframing the pressure. Instead of *Will this meet the requirements of the district?* I think to myself, *Will my student learn something from this?* It's the students who motivate me. And I just need to return to that."
>
> — Jack, 22

Accountability, Autonomy, and Authenticity

The stories these young people tell are clues about how educational leaders can help foster a sense of purpose for and with the students they serve: by finding ways to reframe everyday tasks through accountability, autonomy, and authenticity.

Accountability

Purpose is not just a connection to something bigger, but a sense of responsibility toward that bigger thing. For Hayden, it's band. For Laura, it's ballet. For Jack, it's his students. The stories of these three young people and others highlighted in this report show us ways young people in general are empowered and motivated by the commitment they've made to purpose-filled activities.

And schools can do more to help encourage this sense of accountability, *especially* when framed not just as an obligation to the prevailing standards of success but as a duty to the purpose itself. Only about half (52%) of students agree or strongly agree that "I am needed at this school both in the classroom and out." Nearly the same (53%) say, "I play an important role in my clubs, groups, or classrooms." If young people can feel, as Hayden does, that their role is important— both as a member of a group with a mission *and* as an individual contributing meaningfully to that mission—they are connecting with purpose, which will bolster their mental health. Our data demonstrate a strong and significant correlation between a sense of being needed at school and flourishing in mental health. The more a young person feels needed, the more mentally healthy they tell us they are.

"I am needed at this school both in the classroom and out."

How much would you say you are flourishing in your mental or emotional well-being?

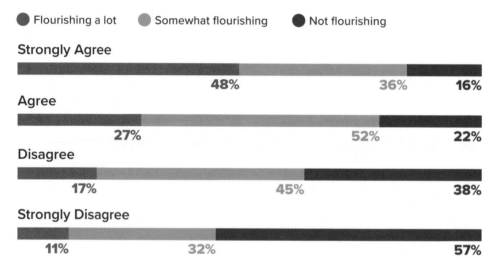

● Flourishing a lot   ● Somewhat flourishing   ● Not flourishing

Strongly Agree

48%   36%   16%

Agree

27%   52%   22%

Disagree

17%   45%   38%

Strongly Disagree

11%   32%   57%

Tide-Turning Tip

Spend time on the questions. Young people say that the activities that best help them discover a sense of purpose are asking questions and exploring new ideas. Amid curriculum requirements, carve out 10 to 15 minutes a week to practice and model the art of good question-asking. This could be stream-of-consciousness journaling with an open-ended prompt, group reflection among classmates, or quick responses to a weekly email that invites the young people to pay closer attention to the movements of their own interests and passions and, importantly, to begin feeling a responsibility toward exploring those questions.

Autonomy

Finding ways to encourage students' autonomy is important for helping them discover and connect with a sense of purpose; it is the difference between passive participation and real engagement. When we asked young people about the kinds of activities that help them discover a sense of purpose, the top four responses they gave—asking questions, trying new things, experiencing hardship, and solving problems—had a common thread. They are instances when a young person is not only connecting with something bigger than themselves but, in doing so, is discovering something about *themselves* at the same time.

What experiences have helped or are currently helping you discover your purpose?

(Young people could select more than one response.)

Asking questions and seeking information about things that matter to me
43%

Developing my interests and talents by trying things and receiving encouragement from others
41%

Experiencing trauma, hardship, or illness, either of my own or someone I care about
39%

Taking action to solve problems that I see by volunteering, protesting, or engaging in other forms of activism
38%

Making music or art
30%

Being inspired by what someone I look up to is doing with their life
27%

Traveling, camping, or hiking in nature or in places with different cultures than my own
20%

Participating in a religious/spiritual community that supports young people as leaders and helps them to learn more about their faith/religion/spirituality
17%

Amirah, a 21-year-old we spoke with for this report, was encouraged to explore a new activity—making art, which, she insisted at first, was not something she could or would usually do. Not only did she discover a new and meaningful activity, but she discovered a new part of herself:

"I was a freshman, and I was going to class and saw a sign that said 'art therapy.' And I was like, *Okay, this is interesting*, but I didn't have time, so I came back after class and I was like, *What is this?* And the therapist was like, *Oh yeah, this is just like an open space.* **Anybody can stop by and you can do anything that's art related.** And I was like, **Okay, but I'm not artistic.** And they were like, *It's okay. You don't have to be.* And so I started going. It was every Wednesday, and I would go, and it was just like, thinking about, it just brings me so much calmness, but it really helped. . . . Now my room is decorated with a bunch of artwork."

—Amirah, 21

Tide-Turning Tip

Offer choice. Whether you are a teacher, a professor, or an administrator, find ways to offer students choice, at least to some degree, to study what interests them. This choice could take place during class selection or within individual classrooms. The goal, however you implement it, is to let students have the autonomy to focus on their interests, which will enhance their ability to internalize what they are learning and give them an opportunity to connect it to their sense of purpose.

Authenticity

Feeling stressed and overwhelmed are common experiences for young people at school. This isn't because they don't *know* what it takes to succeed. Often, the expectations are clear and the tools to succeed are available. But the stress (and the toll on mental health) may actually be related to purpose. When narratives about success are not authentically aligned with a young person's sense of purpose, a young person is more likely to feel overwhelmed and stressed than to experience growth.

This doesn't mean *every* task has to be suited to each individual student's passions and purpose. But consistent efforts to make connections to their sense of authenticity can make a huge difference. Young people know this too. Sixty-six percent of students say, "I feel that the more fully I am myself at school, the more likely I will achieve my goals." If they are invited—their whole, authentic self—to the tasks and activities of their education, they sense that they will be more successful in life. We know the inverse is true too: mental health suffers when the pathways for "purpose" in a school are too narrowly focused on things like academics or athletics.

Young people don't just *need* schools to help them discover a sense of purpose. They *expect* it. Sixty-five percent of young people say, "School is a place where I can ask questions and explore so that I can find my purpose in life." (Recall that asking questions is the activity students rate highest for helping them in this discovery.) The same percentage of students feel that their teachers actively help them do this, with 65% saying, "My teachers notice what I'm good at and encourage me in those directions."

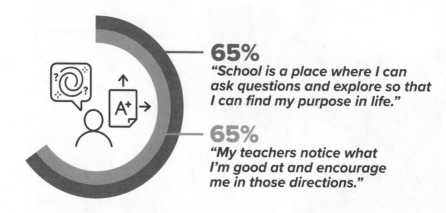

65%
"School is a place where I can ask questions and explore so that I can find my purpose in life."

65%
"My teachers notice what I'm good at and encourage me in those directions."

Tide-Turning Tip

Think outside the classroom. Students tell us that they are not interested in doing things that don't seem to matter. While academics certainly *do* matter, schools have more to offer young people than coursework. *Greater Good Magazine*'s article "How to Help Teens Find Purpose" (2015) presents many excellent resources and insights for educators focused on helping students develop a sense of purpose, many of which are useful beyond just the teen years. Experiential learning through study abroad, service, outdoor curriculum, and contemplative retreats can help young people feel *more* engaged in the classroom after connecting that content to their life outside of school.

Schools are critical sites of formation for young people seeking purpose in life. They provide opportunities to engage young people in conversations about purpose—conversations that, for decades, have been left to home life or religious institutions. Teachers and other adults can help young people cultivate a sense of purpose by reframing school pressures through the lenses of accountability, autonomy, and authenticity. This work sets them up for mental resilience. It can help create a mental-health friendly environment from the ground up at schools. In other words, this work is an organizational mission. In this sense, it exemplifies what it encourages in students themselves.

"... I try reframing the pressure. Instead of, Will this meet the requirements of the district? I think to myself, Will my student learn something from this? It's the students who motivate me. And I just need to return to that."

—Jack, 22

"I don't particularly see myself as someone who has to have a specific goal or who finds myself being someone who has a life that's like, *Oh, I can't believe I'm not doing anything meaningful.* I mean, I find it fulfilling just to be happy."

— Paisley, 18

CONCLUSION

In the 1850s, London was experiencing an epidemic of a different kind: widespread cholera. These outbreaks were all too common at the time— thousands of people had already lost their lives in just the first half of the century, and while the people most affected were poor, nobody was immune.

Theories abounded at the time about what was causing the outbreak, even as doctors and health officials raced to treat victims and save lives. Famously, John Snow, a physician, mapped the cases in Soho, and realized that they clustered around one water pump on Broad Street, where people gathered daily to have their basic needs met, not compromised. He removed the pump handle so that citizens couldn't access the contaminated water, singlehandedly ending the outbreak in that part of the city.

The current mental-health crisis among America's youth is not unlike the epidemic London faced in the 1800s: Nobody is immune. Some are impacted disproportionately. And so many of our resources are dedicated to helping treat victims of the rampant disease that the work of tracing the illness to its source is rarely as urgent. Indeed, it seems like too big a problem for any one person or organization to fix.

When we start to map the "cases" of mental-health issues among young people, we see various clusters—including a significant cluster during the ages when they are likely in school. Schools are, to be sure, at the forefront of responding creatively to the mental-health crisis. But like the water pump on Broad Street, as young people gather at this resource daily, it also inevitably becomes a hub that intensifies their exposure to illness.

This report hopes to reflect the innovation that Dr. John Snow showed in the nineteenth century. We can look not just to care for the suffering but also to the conditions that cause that suffering in the first place. We can build our schools to be mental-health friendly rather than just responsive when people get sick. We can find simple ways to ward off disease before it starts, like snapping the handle off a water pump, creating opportunities for connection, helping align expectations and tools, and incorporating simple strategies to encourage a sense of purpose in students.

But we want to go one step further than Snow. Rather than stop the flow of contaminated water, we want to filter the water and distribute it widely. We want to help schools to avoid missteps in mental-health advocacy, and to become spaces conducive to mental health and flourishing for all young people.

APPENDIX
Research Methodology & Promise

Quantitative Research

Springtide Research Institute collects quantitative data through surveys and qualitative data through interviews. The quantitative data tell us what is happening. The qualitative data tell us why and how it is happening.

For the quantitative data in this report, we conducted a dedicated study about mental health in educational settings beginning in the fall of 2021. We surveyed a nationally representative sample of young people ages 13 to 25 in the United States, totaling 4,038 participants. The sample was weighted for age, gender, race, and region to match the demographics of the country, and it produces a margin of error of +/- 3%. The age, gender, and racial demographics of this sample are indicated in the tables on the right.

Age	Valid Percent
13 to 17	22%
18 to 25	78%
Total	100%

Gender	Valid Percent
Girl/Woman or Transgender Girl/Woman	56%
Boy/Man or Transgender Boy/Man	39%
Nonbinary	4%
Total	100%

Race	Valid Percent
White	51%
Hispanic or Latino	22%
Black or African American	19%
American Indian or Alaska Native	1%
Asian	6%
Native Hawaiian / Pacific Islander	>1%
Other	2%
Total	100%

Tables may not add up to exactly 100% due to rounding.

Qualitative Research

For the qualitative research, we conducted 80 in-depth interviews, either in person, via telephone, or via video. Interviews focused on understanding how young people regard and experience mental health in their lives, specifically in an educational setting. Conversations were guided but open-ended, allowing for as much direction as possible from the interviewee. Interviews were transcribed, lightly cleaned, and then analyzed thematically. The use of brackets in the qualitative quotes indicates that a word was replaced. All replacements come directly from the context of the quote to ensure accuracy. The use of bold in the qualitative quotes indicates emphasis added rather than emphasis in the original.

In addition to the interviews, we hosted a focus group in a ninth-grade classroom of 24 students. The conversation took place in December 2021 and lasted about 90 minutes. Our researchers asked students to take time to record their thoughts and to share aloud their responses to questions about mental health in their school environment.

Interviews and survey responses are confidential, and all names of research participants in this report are pseudonyms. For more information, please contact us at research@springtideresearch.org.

Our Research Promise

At Springtide Research Institute, we are committed to a Data with Heart™ approach. Our approach is rooted in deep systematic listening to young people and the things they care about. It is founded on values, commitments, and beliefs that ground why we do our research, in addition to employing a variety of rigorous qualitative and quantitative methods. Our philosophy and approach are dynamic— informed by varying ways of listening to young people through our Springtide Ambassadors Program (SAP), Writer in Residence, *The Voices of Young People Podcast*, interns, and BIPOC fellows.

This series of commitments is ever-evolving, just like the diversity and context of the young people that we are committed to. We commit to reassessing this philosophy in an ongoing capacity to reflect and embody our promise to be culturally informed and inclusive.

1. We are committed to listening to young people.

2. We believe that the voices of young people should shape what we study.

3. We bring our whole selves into our conversations with young people to build trust by owning our biases, being vulnerable about our own lives, and demonstrating that we are accountable for what we do and do not know.

4. We strive to deepen our understanding of young people, rather than impose our expectations on them.

5. We encourage young people to share their stories and creative expressions because we recognize that knowledge and truth are culturally bound and that young people actively shape our world.

6. We understand the value of numbers and that they are enriched by the words shared with us by young people.

7. We know that the questions are just as important as the answers and that our inquiry itself is a statement of our values.

8. We seek to break down the boxes that research often puts people into by exploring and understanding the highly variable lived experiences of young people.

9. We foster diverse ways of understanding the nuance and complexity of young people and social phenomena and are constantly expanding our methodologies to reflect what we have learned.

10. We resolve to produce knowledge that is actionable, useful, and valuable to the communities and organizations we serve.

Note: Numerals above are for reference only and not an indication of priority.

ACKNOWLEDGMENTS

Created by the publishing team of Springtide Research Institute.

Printed in the United States of America
#5937
ISBN 978-1-64121-179-6

Research Team

Josh Packard, PhD, Executive Director

Megan Bissell, MA, Head of Research

Nabil Tueme, MA, Associate Researcher

Jaclyn Doherty, MA, Researcher

Kari Koshiol, PhD, Researcher

Adrianna Smell, MA, Researcher

Writing Team

Ellen Koneck, MAR, Head of Writing & Editing

Josh Packard, PhD, Executive Director

Maura Thompson Hagarty, PhD, Developmental Editor

Kari Koshiol, PhD, Contributing Writer

Hannah Connors, Springtide Writing Fellow

Creative Design and Production Team

Steven Mino

Sigrid Lindholm

Brooke Saron

Becky Gochanour

Our Thanks

We offer special thanks to the Springtide Research Advisory Board, a group of practitioners and experts from wide-ranging fields. They provided guidance on how Springtide might contribute to a conversation on mental health and Gen Z, oriented our work through a robust board meeting in fall 2021, and shared individual expertise that shaped aspects of this report.

Special thanks, as well, to the 2021 and 2022 cohorts of the Springtide Ambassadors Program. They have been regular conversation partners about mental health and Gen Z. They responded to surveys about possible focus areas and engaged in dialogue about questions and themes that arose in the course of our research and writing.

The influence of both groups in this report is diffuse and substantial. Their voices are clear in the two "A Closer Look" features, in our language, and in some of our insights and conclusions.

References

Works Cited

Page 10 – The excerpt about the critical role of educators is from the website Inseparable, *inseparable.us/hopeful-futures.*

Page 28 – The quotation about people with more frequent contacts is from Allan V. Horwitz, "An Overview of Sociological Perspectives on the Definitions, Causes, and Response to Mental Health and Illness," *A Handbook for the Study of Mental Health: Social Contexts, Theories, and Systems* (Cambridge: Cambridge University Press, 2009), 10.

Works Consulted

American Academy of Pediatrics. "AAP-AACAP-CHA Declaration of a National Emergency in Child and Adolescent Mental Health." *aap.org/en/advocacy/child-and-adolescent-healthy-mental-development/aap-aacap-cha-declaration-of-a-national-emergency-in-child-and-adolescent-mental-health/.*

Appelrouth, Scott, and Laura Desfor Edles. *Classical & Contemporary Sociological Theory.* 4th ed. Los Angeles: Sage, 2021.

Calhoun, Craig, ed. Robert K. Merton: *Sociology of Science and Sociology as Science.* New York: Columbia University Press, 2010.

Centers for Disease Control and Prevention. "Schools Start Too Early." *cdc.gov/sleep/features/schools-start-too-early.html.*

Durkheim: *amazon.com/Classical-Social-Theory-Modern-Society-ebook/dp/B00SPNHBGK/ref=sr_1_1?crid=128IN-WTWFE6ZM&keywords=Durkheim+reader&qid=1647633015&sprefix=durkheim+reader%2Caps%2C117&sr=8-1*

Horwitz, Allan V. "An Overview of Sociological Perspectives on the Definitions, Causes, and Response to Mental Health and Illness," *A Handbook for the Study of Mental Health: Social Contexts, Theories, and Systems.* Cambridge: Cambridge University Press, 2009.

Inseparable. "Hopeful Futures Campaign: America's School Mental Health Report Card." February 2022. *hopefulfutures.us/wp-content/uploads/2022/02/Final_Master_021522.pdf.*

Merton: *amazon.com/Robert-K-Merton-Sociology-Columbia-ebook/dp/B0064CZ11Q/ref=sr_1_4?crid=23IB9K-KT4RX9A&keywords=%22Robert+merton%22+reader&qid=1647632786&sprefix=robert+merton+reader%2Caps%2C84&sr=8-4*

Merton: *amazon.com/Classical-Contemporary-Sociological-Theory-Readings-dp-1506387993/dp/1506387993/ref=dp_ob_title_bk?asin=1506387993&revisionId=&format=4&depth=1*

Richtel, Matt. "Surgeon General Warns of Youth Mental Health Crisis." *New York Times.* December 7, 2021. *nytimes.com/2021/12/07/science/pandemic-adolescents-depression-anxiety.html.*

Royce, Edward. *Classical Social Theory and Modern Society: Marx, Durkheim, Weber.* New York: Rowan & Littlefield, 2015.

Photo Credits

(All photos appear on Unsplash unless otherwise indicated.)

Pages 2–3 Michael Pfister

Cover and pages 8, 15, 26, 42, 56, and 70 Chuttersnap

Cover and pages 8, 26, 42, and 56 Minh Ngọc

Cover and pages 8, 26, 42, and 56 Renan Kamikoga

Cover and pages 8, 26, 42, and 56 Monkey Business Images (Shutterstock)

Cover and pages 8, 26, 42, and 56 Marius Masalar

Cover and pages 8, 15, 26, 42, and 56 Desiray Green

Page 15 Hatham Eafs

Page 15 Fa Barboza

Page 15 Tyson

Page 15 ergonofis

Pages 15 and 70 Frantisek Duris

Pages 15 and 70 Sora Khan

Pages 15 and 70 CDC

Pages 25 Kyle Gregory Devaras

Page 39 Brooke Cagle

Page 55 Austin Pacheco

Page 65 Rifqi Ali Ridho

Page 70 Eyoel Kahssay

Springtide Research Institute publications are supported by organizations, foundations, and readers like you. We are deeply grateful for all these levels of partnership and support.

Are you interested in supporting future publications?

For more information, contact Donna Van Pelt, Director of Foundation Relations, at *donna@springtideresearch.org*.

Custom research for mission-driven organizations.

Move your organization forward, confidently.

Springtide offers custom research to help you learn more so you can do more.

Our research services include program evaluation, grant support, custom surveys and data collection, and more. In addition, Dr. Josh Packard is available for presentations on Springtide data or the custom research you commission.

Contact Megan at *research@springtideresesarch.org* or visit *springtideresearch.org/custom-research* to learn more.

Program Evaluation

Grant Support

Custom Surveys

Data Collection

OUR MISSION

Compelled by the urgent desire to listen and attend to the lives of young people (ages 13 to 25), Springtide Research Institute is committed to understanding the distinct ways new generations experience and express community, identity, and meaning.

We exist at the intersection of religious and human experience in the lives of young people. And we're here to listen.

We combine quantitative and qualitative research to reflect and amplify the lived realities of young people as they navigate shifting social, cultural, and religious landscapes. Delivering fresh data and actionable insights, we equip those who care about young people to care better.

Stay in Touch

Visit the Springtide website for a variety of resources to help you support the young people in your life, including podcasts, blogs, video series, and our other reports and books. Find these resources and sign up for our biweekly newsletter, *The Tide Report*, at *springtideresearch.org*.

Join the conversation, and connect with us on social media.
Follow **@WeAreSpringtide** on Facebook, Instagram, and Twitter.

Share how you're building innovative ways to help young people flourish and find balance in work and in life. Send us a note at *stories@springtideresearch.org*.